Un Tour d'

Also by David Kinloch

Dustie-Fute
Paris Forfar

DAVID KINLOCH

Un Tour d'Ecosse

For Richard
– who helped me make
some of these poems
better! With thanks
from David

June 6th, 2001

CARCANET

Published in Great Britain in 2001 by
Carcanet Press Limited
4th Floor, Conavon Court
12–16 Blackfriars Street
Manchester M3 5BQ

A CIP catalogue record for this book
is available from the British Library

ISBN 1 85754 516 8

The publisher acknowledges financial assistance
from the Arts Council of England

Set in Monotype Garamond by XL Publishing Services, Tiverton
Printed and bound in England by SRP Ltd, Exeter

For Eric

Acknowledgements

Some of these poems have appeared in the following publications: *Big Allis* (USA), *Cutting Teeth*, *Edinburgh Review*, *Etudes écossaises* (France), *Mirage* (USA), *Gay Love Poetry: An Anthology* (ed. Neil Powell, Robinson, 1997), *New Writing Scotland*, *PN Review*, *The Rialto*, *Samizdat* (USA), *Skinklin' Star*, *Southfields*, *La Traductière* (France), *Verse, Unknown is Best: a Celebration of Edwin Morgan at Eighty* (ed. Robyn Marsack and Hamish Whyte, Mariscat Press and Scottish Poetry Library, 2000), *Without Day: Proposals for a Scottish Parliament* (ed. Alec Finlay, Polygon: Pocketbooks, 2000).

The two poems entitled 'from *The Year of the Dragon*' are translated from Emmanuel Moses, 'L'Année du dragon', *Les Bâtiments de la compagnie asiatique* (Obsidian, 1993).

'To A Bardie' and 'Casting a Line' are contributions to a multimedia celebration of the New York poet, Frank O'Hara, which played at venues in Scotland and the North of England before being performed at the *CCA* (Glasgow) as part of the 1997 MayFest. It was entitled *On Your Nerve*, and was co-written with W.N. Herbert and Donny O'Rourke.

'Bed' was made into a short film for the 1998 'Glasgay!' Festival and the Glasgow Film and Video Workshop.

Some of the epigraphs in the 'Tour d'Ecosse' sequence are quoted, with the permission of the author, from Josée Lapeyrère's *Comment faire le Tour: Eloge de la Course* (Point Hors Ligne, 1992).

THANKS

in particular to some skilful readers and friends: Richard, Donny, David and Bill.

Contents

CUSTOMS

Saicret

It begins with paper: a love of shoe box tissue vaguely marked with the shape of shoes, the rice paper of a box camera collecting shadows, a huge sheet thrown across couch and armchair through which you peer, as through a Japanese shoji, turning down the volume of the daylight, erasing the contours of your mother: 'Ssh! Can ye no keep a saicret!'

A little later you become a misplaced marker in a book about an imaginary Asian childhood, a wandering margin, never in the same place twice, covering traces. There, you discover an odd talent for shadow boxing on the walls of bedrooms on hot nights in the monsoon. You are pure moonshine. An endless game of patience. Of *Risk*. Or you are a cloud on caran d'ache, a difference just barely visible. They have to X-ray you twice.

Then today, on Capri, you look within the corolla of a roadside woadwaxen and, in its distance, find a stamen round and black as Lenin's bowler hat which he wears to exiled chess with Gorky. Pawn to King four: chessmen move like insects and cast brief shadows on the petal wall. You squeeze the stamen and it stains your fingers an inky blue, returning you to paper: note the Amalfi watermark – thought a rarity – a sea-side empire of old secrets glimmering through coral parchment.

The Snuffmill

In the 'little-bud-moon'
Braves truffled through
Linn Forest: Occaneechi
Of Virginia with our bows
And feathers, we whooped
The weir until it reached

The ruined snuffmill of Cathcart.
Then our sneezes jitter-
Bugged with laughter
Round the canyon walls.
At tea-time we went home
And forgot. Until a firework

Party on a midnight lawn
When Boggles planted
Sparklers in my hair
Proclaiming me the Queen
Of Halloween and I thought
Precociously how fire

Tickling night air
Was like the snuff
That convulsed rich
Ancestors of my hosts.
But then the snuffmill
Sank again, unvisited,

While I grew up to study
The Enlightenment
And found imagination
Was memory, chat, sneeze and gurgle
Of a pebbled burn, snot-marked
Ferns, dank millstones, iridescent stuff.

Clairvoyance

My father hovers in a corner
Of *The Clairvoyance Shop,*
Unsure if he's a ghost or not.

Shrouded in a fug of nicotine
And Jesus props, a fat medium
Fastidiously inhales, then nods

And speaks the words
I've given Dad a hundred times
In thought since he passed

Over. They spool back
Those moments on the couch
When Mum slumped down

Beside us, barely whispering
How he 'just turned to me
And breathed out' and I

Breathed deeply in,
Knowing I could speak, have sex,
Become the Papist poof

He'd slated in his cups.
Now Fatman's cockney cup
Tells me Dad is proud of me:

'My weakness has become your strength.
You're twice the man I ever was.'
The Kipling mode rings true,

As does the Brain of Britain
Score he gives me for my life
So far: 8/10. Not bad. And those

Deducted points? If I *had* spoken
It would have killed him
And he'd be alive today.

Wi his dicky-bow

fae the French o Josée Lapeyrère

Wi his dicky-bow black as a
keeker the ref jigs
hauns still as deid mackerel
fists scrunched as a stane
aboot the boxers ach! his 'BREAK!'

unties their clinch
– 'YER AS SLAW AS A WEE
LASSIE MAN' – widny they
jist each o the two o them
jist luv tae banjo
the crap-bag an puntie-up
owre the ither side aw
cockie-like but

it's the huggin stoaps em
lumberin the ither's airms
cheek fur chowl their big
rid gloves are Mickey's ears
aw bloody aboot the gills an oan
the sheen o the sassenach's shouder

an the daurk behind the cords
o the ring hotchin wi faces:
'HAW COCKYNUT-HEID
DINNAE JIST STAUN THER
LIKE A FART IN A TRANCE
WEE MASIE SEYS GET TORE

IN MELT THE BUGGER' ah luv
tae see yon douce hardman
yon big stumer o a mainiger
wi his saft jessie hauns
his shuge yeller sponge
his gob in the lug o the
boxer close up close up
a wheesht a caress
'screw the nut oan ye go get steamed right intae him'

Glossary

keeker – black eye; *banjo* – to hit someone a very hard, single blow; *crap-bag* – a coward, *puntie-up* – to climb onto or over something; *lumber* – to 'get off with' someone; *hotchin* – busy; *stumer* – a fool; *lug* – ear; *screw the nut* – calm down.

from *The Year of the Dragon*

Translated from the French of Emmanuel Moses

Here is bread – Lugano – the wine of the stars.
Angels sitting beside water tell the stories of their lives,
Sodom, the struggle with the shepherd until daybreak.

You will remain there, beside those seeking something else
Beneath the shape of flower or bird. Already
The dream train puffs its way forward. Already,

In the roof of the umbrella, a piece of gold glitters: *la vie nouvelle.*
Like that evening we walked back along the road to Cologny
With the sun trained on our backs. Let us play chess with the seasons:

Winter, black queen, takes the white castle of Autumn. It had to be so.
A deer has collapsed in the snow. Hunters found it one morning,
Touched by the shadow of a bullet. On this festive day, it was quite
proper

Someone should make a speech, so he opened his mouth and the year
Began under the sign of miracles and contraband coffee. Here is an
eagle
Transformed into a man, a man who tells you as much about it as he
knows

Stand where I can see you, in the light that sings like a cricket.
A new day is born in the entrails of this night.

Aye. Pause. Ah said pause. Och fuck it! Ye're past it. Past it! Rewind!
What? Aye. Just tryin. Tryin tae get the shot. In focus like. Difficult
what with the grainy downslide. But ye've goat tae try. Hit the button.
Jeezus! Naw! It wizny him. But somewun, some*thin*. Look ye can see
him. Through the spray. Just. Yon adam's apple. The hollow at the
base. Bone coloured skin. Aye aw skin an bone he wiz. Feathery hair.
Aye ah'm the cropped wan. Och fur speed, jimmy! Fur speed! Whit
d'you think! Hit the button fur chrissake. He pushed *ma* button ah kin
tell ye! Pain. Ecstasy. Aw wun in'it? *We* know that! Aye. That's it! Tha's
it! Is that a... Christ! It's a fuckin claw! Ah've been tangoin wi a bear!
Naw, mair like a cat! What a bitch! Scream or cum? Below the belt
anyway. Below the fuckin belt. God ah wiz goodlookin in them days.
Even wi ma gob open! Squirmin. He knew it, jealous bastard. Och
look at the slaw-motion tear. Hold yer finger oan it. Constant-like. Aye
well. Ah'm jist numb now. It's all over. Has been fur years. Now and
again ah rewind. Try tae catch that moment when ah wiz forced tae
chynge, get a life. When ah woke up in hoaspital they undid the straps
and ah coudny remember a thing. No even ma name. But the pain,
the fuckin pain! An ache in ma crotch the size ae a cuntry.

Accommodations

'Just a bivouac' we agreed,
'Provisional', though I suspect
The 'vision' part was clear
In our minds as the glacier
Tipping Glasgow down
From Hampden Terrace,
Frosting it towards the Campsies:

The *nous* to keep it so,
A sharing encamped among
Acres of Mum's ex-velour
And springless sofas
Or those blue satin drapes
I once dressed up in like a sari
Until Dad scorned me off to bed;

Accommodations, like that of
Mrs Anne McCafferty's Corner Shop
Whose shades are patterned
With Punjabi suns cast by next
Door's Deli: 'Assalaam
alaikum' 'Vaalaikum
Salaam' drifts up through
Sparkling zebra crossings.

Now, in late solstice twilight,
Firefly Belisha Beacons christmas
The decanted football pitch
Which waves like a dark
Green sheet hung
In New Gorbals, waves
Me, like *Sanashan
Textiles'* magic carpet,

Back through our bookmarked
B and B's, the best of all the wests
We've travelled through, and
Forward, foraging our future
For the house that we'll endow
Together; it lurches
From this tug of war as the slap
Of closing shop fronts

Could be shutters, obumbrated
Slats whose pitted varnish
Mottles the reflection of your
Face that's gone Barbadan
In the sunlight.
Shanty and plimsoled
You heat baked beans
And kiss me in a slow black voice,

A voice the colour of a tenor
Sax that steams out hand in
Hand with showers of sex
To mingle with the miles
Below of Po Plain mist
Besieging bathroom tiles.
From there an outdoor spiral
Staircase is always twisting

Down to Crail and berry
Picking gardens which then spring
Up to pink verandas slung
Beneath a tree so sage
It has become the house itself.
Once through those jalousies
Your taste confers Chambordish
Dados everywhere and Bach

Is running everything. But I'm
Content to settle in the echo
Of the green pool's sheen,
The hum of distant traffic,
Drum beats, the husky murmur
Of a 'Good Morning, Paul',
All holding, for the space of that poised
Phrase, the world barely at abeyance…

Pull back the shutters' slats again
Until they're horizontal, become
The wooden drying board
Of the Lamlash sink they bathed you in
When you were two; there we'll be
Just dishes among the dishes,
Giggling through the rainbow
Suds of a freezing Arran cottage,

Grow up together, never have lived
Apart. Wood whorls rev
Up the shutters, tiny
Tornadoes, knotting memory,
Desire; twisters, they
Jump before my eyes

And I am home again
To find 'Morocco' by Matisse
Is now 'Tangiers' by Morocco.
My stopped clock has acquired
Fake chimes by Louis Quinze.
I wince, you smile and we
Hopscotch on the dappled
Paving of our eazy-ozy inscapes.

Weather moved you in with me:
A freeze so great the pipes of Stenhousemuir
Refused to sing and you became Glaswegian.
Reports confirm that I was not at home
That night, a night Jack stoked his lungs
And shivered timbers, huffed and puffed
And blew your house right down.

from *The Year of the Dragon*

Translated from the French of Emmanuel Moses

I won't forget your bus-shaped dragons, London,
Nor the storks beneath the Saint-Charles Bridge, one April evening…

Elegy suits homecomings.
In the kitchen, a smell of death escapes from the fridge.

The greetings card slipped under the door
Is to a total stranger.

Your mouth still tastes of damp wood and tarmac.
Last night, Benedict jumped from my dream to yours,

Spilling onto the pillow a little Sicilian earth.
You open the case where the books sleep.

You're not so wild about my
Latest poems, why deny it?

A line of Donne on the stars and you plunge
Into your herbal bath, warding off a cold.

In Brompton Cemetery

A patter of squirrel
feet fall like rain
across the tombs

and spirit my
glance to *Prince
Bibesco*. Moss

unletters his name,
so many half
caught: *widow*

of, infant, dearly.
Grass ears fritter
away and offer

occasional unknown
wild-flowers, the
tangled dark

at the bole of trees,
half a bench
fraying into shadow.

Pigeons examining
my feet are far
from ghosts

And only Richard
Tauber's grave
sings against

forgetfulness,
bedecked in pansies,
the high C

of a single iris.

*

Lichens resist
each note we strike here,
the true tenor of it:

just web and brief
silver, the beaten body
of the earth.

A strafe of
melon seeds pave you
to the picket fence

of a white
quiet canton
and the RIP boys

aged 21 or 23 who
served, defended, rest.
Other ones pad by

outside in designer
names that flare
the cemetery blur,

ignite the spokes
of lycrad cyclists
who lap them, alight

among unconsecrated
colonnades and await
the tryst. Pot-bellies

amble their desire
among the athletes
and here the game

of seek and seek
begins: a lithe muscle
suns its walkman on a slab:

his silver shades
annealed like salamanders
to his eyes.

A hot breeze uplifts
choruses of stares
across the unkempt stones

and all aches to be fenced
in a corner, asked
for a momentary

name. A little blond
manfully defends
his plot, watches

the slow summer-
stunned bee
crash the asphalt,

shed a wing
and wipe its eyes.

Blade

Crematorium green fields:
An open stride of trees,
Plenty of air for us,
Visiting, waving off

The dead. But you yearn
For the single blade of grass
Among it all that will splice
An unquenchable paper

Cut or the same blade
Held between bleeding fingers
Mimic a raw oboe
Whose exact snide pitch

Will perforate the tympanum
And let you bleed,
Then teach, then eat,
Then sleep and feel it all.

Conversion

A helicopter swings through incensed
Dusk, its tiny light inflaming
Eye of fern, laburnum copse,
Surveying undercover men,
Hard on the hassock of the earth,
Heads bobbing in a fakery of prayer.

Its blades spin round the time
I knelt before a Priest
And changed my faith,
Thief of myself for the sake
Of that friend's hand,
– Its snaking veins of Mary-blue –
Hand job so delicately placed

Upon converting shoulders
I could not face the sideways
Jump, the saving lick
Of the flickering Host who
Stretched a point and dived and
Winked from the tabernacle
Of his in-box.

The Priest in his clover cope
Takes me at crotch level
As his example for the day,
Looks down but only hears
Absent flesh that is really there
Ejaculating a camouflage
Of handshakes,

The kind which welcomed
To his weekly study,
Woodbound for Instruction
Over tea and hot-crossed legs;
The reiterated Benediction:
'And next week remind me
To mention Homosexuality.'

Now I am out on the heath
Examined orally again
Beneath a conference of trees,
Answering, as always,
Slightly beside the point:
'What do you like?'
'What are ye intae?'

I try to recollect myself
But scatter through the copter's
Scythe. Caught in its elysian glow
I cannot see and am not seen
By that white whirring dove,
The deafening response
Of its red, arresting eye.

An Epistle to Robert Burns

*My body too was attacked by that most dreadful distemper, a hypochondria, or
confirmed Melancholy: in this wretched state, [...] I hung my harp on the Willow
tree, except in some lucid intervals, in which I composed the following.*
Robert Burns, *Commonplace Book* (March 1784)

Robert Burns, the harps are on the cypress trees
And melancholia is drowning in the swimming pool,
Your shadow wavers like a Tuscan butterfly
Across its filtered green and a youth,
With your black locks but browner arms,
Rakes out leaves and corpses of mosquitoes.

Robert Burns, I think of you,
Ploughing through the little ice age
Of Mossgiel and Lochlie,
Sodden *fattoria* of the Ayrshire Plains,
While I play Elton – *White Powder, White Lady* –
Supine on the *far niente* of a Capezzano
Lounger, watching the tiny pulse of a gecko's heart
Darting in its throat.

Robert Burns, the only thing we have in common
Is our love of sex, the need to suck
The *sustantificque mouelle* of now
And sing it to the others.
But you can keep the litany of Highland
Maries who you might have fucked
And my fellow poets, your true descendants,
Can make their babies while I spend,
Spend in Tuscany on pasta and Chianti.

Robert Burns, what was the last image
Your eyes closed upon? Mine will be
This horizontal shot of Eric
With a Wilbur Smith raised at 45 degrees,
Sliced by a white board still vibrating
From a dive and then the solitary stumble
Of an ant on terracotta,
Wayward and vernacular as the 'guid black
Prent of Scots', the only thing I envy you.

Robert Burns, when the shade slakes
A quarter of our swimming pool,
I shall take my dip.

The Hunt

One sleepless night,
Stargazing by the flagpole in Queen's Park,
Thugs tried to shaft my neighbour
With his telescope
Sure he was a 'poof'.

He joked himself away,
Regaled us at a Close Meeting
With his close shave,
While I silently recalled
An unforgettable park dusk:
The sound of padding sneakers
On the paths, the reek of over-
Ripe laburnum, poppers in a copse

And the sudden, shaking gallop
Of a mounted cop all caped and
Kaisered, lightbrigading our intense
Brief scatter at an incline
Through the grass, the shrieking

Neigh, the curse and crash,
Then, through the deep blue
Twilight, the wracking sobs
As a figure bent across his ruined
Horse: at my quiet feet
The splayed and helpless animals.

Cyrano in Heiven

fur Edwin Morgan

Jist haud yer hosses Roxane! Ahm awmost ther! Ma plume hes picked the lock o perly gates an ah kin jist mak oot the braw, brent, dark-avised looks o yon Christian fella, yon fair-farrand, swankin kelp who seems jist fine, aye so he does och even if his airms an legs is aw clouds, aw alto-cumulus castellatus an sic like! Aye but can ye no see us now Roxane! He's takin ma rapier haund in his an pumpin it fur auld lang syne. Guid on ye laddie! Aw but ye wer a richt knappy, kibble, winsome biddie so ye wur back then, doon ther in Roxane-land. Whit? Roxane ah said! Ach but ye may be richt… 39 if she wiz a day when ah goat pulleyed up! Anywey, whit say you an me jink back o that nimbo-stratus an tak a wee nip o whitever nectar nutrient is oan tap? Ah find you tae be a cloud uv an ovoid shape wi clean cut edges ah could get used tae so ah could. Your smaa depth, flat base an firm well rounded heads, that anvil fist, the upcurrents o yer thermals, ah could build a heivenly Gascony on! Furst though ah must just post a wee séance doon tae ma cadets: sum vital instructions afore the next batch get despatched up here:

Cyrano's Weather Tips fur Cadets
en route fur Salvatioun

1 Dinnae fly in cumulo-nimbus unless ye cannae avoid it. Them clouds are fur bonnier fae ootside.

2 When divin through 10/10 stratus remember that in the meantime, the cloud may huv taken a dauner doon tae the grun or the grun whisked up tae the cloud.

3 When smoored in snaw-bree dinnae let yer furst thocht be tae get doon. Ye certainly wull if ye dae.

Glossary
braw – handsome; *brent* – smooth, fearless, lofty; *dark-avised* – having dark hair and eyes; *fair-farrand* – handsome; *swankin* – athletic; *kelp* – a big raw-boned youth; *knappy* – sturdy, strong; *kibble* – well-built, agile; *winsome* – charming; *dauner* – stroll; *smoor* – smother, suffocate; *snaw bree* – melted snow or ice.

A Vision of W.S. Graham's Hippopotamus in Venice

Each word is but a longing
  Set out to break from a difficult home.
    W.S. Graham, 'The Nightfishing'

What Graham heard first
Was the matronly chafe
Of her widow udders
On the Algonquin Hotel's
Thick pile; what he saw

Was the swing and the
Prance of her all-
Belly, softer and more velvet
Than the empty, numbered
Corridor; what he sent,

Swimming across Iapetus,
Was this old sea-cow
Now wellingtoned
In Venetian shallows
As real as yellow
Café chairs rafting
Marble and meltwater.

Hippo moons at Byzantine
Domes seeking us
Out of the crowd.
And I pray that – gingerly –
She'll not step up
Onto duckboards
And mince our way…
But she does
And the city sinks at last.

I am lagooned in silence
Until the lapping torches
Nuzzling Palazzi stairs dive
Down like bell anemone
And phosphoresce the green.

And then through the flood
I hear the slightly panicked
Whirr of castagnetting hippo
Feet as they lose their grip
And power churn the water-burn

Down to me: her skirts of flesh
Bulge out, her piggy blue
Mosaic eyes and Pantactrator
Face, benevolent as Mary
Poppins, peer out at me.

She seems to speak
A delicate fossil tongue
And tells me it's the one
Will buoy me up again
And recreate the stones of Venice.

So we dredge the sludge
Of Istrian effluent, dodge
Drowning ducal piles
And make our treasure-chest
Discovery beneath the cemetery isle:

A cache of language
Beneath the Fondamenta,
Waterlogged parchments
Of Scottish glossaries
Plugging the solid caranto:

Here is dull broach of
Lion drenched in a
Summer-sob, there a
Map of *water-gaw*
Where it all began again.

But her hooves crunch over
The coralled etymologies:
Ruined horny grapolites
That only once caught sense
In tiny comb-like sieves.

Here is a stash of *utteridge*
Strewn and *unmensefu,*
The *undersook*
Of 'Sestieri': a *sumphie*
Stour-o'-Words.

There is *maroonjous* pine
That Gritti and Ca Rezonnico
Deliquesce upon, the water-
Slain-moss that peats their roots
And eats their damp-proof stone.

Oh for a *neid-fire*
To ignite canals
Electrify a doge of sound
That would convoke
The glittering, *dowie* signifiers.

I turn in the *wallowa*
Turn to hippo in the *wallowae,*
But she's slipped aloft already,
A 'cathédrale engloutie'
Burbling on her mobile.

I wonder in the *howe-dumb-deid*
Beneath the 'canalazzo'
Wonder at that hoof
Of *umbersorrow* lit
By the lagoon's blue day,
Wonder what my hippo
Is using me for.

Glossary

summer-sob – frequent slight rains in summer; *water-gaw* – the fragment of a rainbow appearing in the horizon; seen in the north or east, a sign of bad weather, *utteridge* – utterance, power of speech; *unmensefu* – disorderly; unbecoming; indiscreet; used of weather: rough, unseasonable; *undersook* – an undercurrent flowing against that on the surface; *sumphie* – stupid, foolish; sulky, sullen; *stour-o'-words* – a wordy discourse; *maroonjous* – harsh, sturdy; *neid-fire* – fire produced from the friction of two pieces of wood; a beacon-fire, also used to express the phosphoric light of rotten wood, *dowie* – sad, mournful, inclined to decay; *wallow/ae* – an exclamation of sorrow, the devil; *howe-dumb-deid* – used of night, the middle, when silence reigns; *umbersorrow* – surliness, resisting disease or the effects of bad weather.

To a Bardie

fae a cockroach, on jumping out of a New York fridge and confronting him, July 1997

The cockroaches like nuggets half hid in the bran
Frank O'Hara, 'Alma'

Huge, baldit, chitterin, timrous bardie,
Openin the fridge wiz richt fuhardie!
Weel micht ye fart awa ma lairdie
　　Wi 'Christ, a cockroach!'
I wad jist luv tae rin an chase thee
　　Wi murd'ring reproach!

Welcome tae ma sweltrin bothy,
This liftless scraper, clammy, growthie.
It cracks me up tae see you drouthy.
　　Tough! Ahv drunk the beer,
Munched the bran O'Hara slipped sae poofy-
　　Like in here.

Which pairts wad ye hae me play? James Dean?
Your frien fancied him enough, the lean
Cute, saft smoulder o his outcast een
　　Jessie rebel!
Whit cause is worth a nicht i' mean
　　Cockroach hotel?!

Aye right! Ma Bronx bodywork's a smash
In motion, ma brow a buckled dash
Board, twitchin, sniffin the stashed hash
　　O ma guid cousin,
Hit n'run gekko wi Groucho tache,
　　Corlione's chin.

Or wad it be Ginger, wee Tom Cruise
Pas de deuxing wi Mel whose fuse
Is too short fur his kilt! You choose!
　　Brief Encounter?
No brief enough fur me, sae muse
　　On Lana Turner!

You'd like tae find a symbol in me:
N'this dreich hole ahm Cocteau's repartee,
Fleur du mal sookin up the ennui
        O bein you,
Core o the Big Aipple's bel esprit.
        Twad mak me spew!

Frank grew oot o this an aw the folk
He toasted wi his can o coke,
Grace, Patsy, Warren, Kenneth Koch
        Suffered nae sea-change,
Risin fae Fire Island waves, soaked,
        Mair themsels, strange.

Jist a cockroach in a New York fridge
You've writ a poem tae, nae bridge
Tae sumfin bigger an masel, abridged
        Myth, camp and free.
You're the wan gaes on his nerve, on edge,
        In tongues, no me.

Glossary
bothy – a makeshift hut; *growthie* – warm and moist; *drouthy* – thirsty; *een* – eyes.

Casting a Line

'Tu soulèveras le rideau
Et maintenant voila que s'ouvre la fenêtre'
Wrote the poet Guillaume Apollinaire
In the world's first 'poème conversation'
'You will lift up the curtain
And now here is the window opening'
Which I did and it does
Amid blue potato-printed walls
Of Columba's Hotel, Loch Fyne
'Tu souleveras le rideau'

On fat Guillaume himself
Casting a mean line from the century's
Turn beneath the barking Tarbert
Gulls O Albert Vladimir Apollinaris de
Kostrowitsky 'Paris Vancouver Hyères
Maintenon New York et les Antilles'
Shiver in circles where your bait schlocks
In and a *tour eiffel* of sea-weed
Corrugates beneath your bum!
Trout browse his boat like *bouquinistes*
And as his body signs a whirligig
Of cedar, oak-wood, russet, moonlight
Oars nailed to the peely-wally
Canvas of his face he hooks
The cubist eye-browed fish
And tenderly throws them
Back.

'Tu soulèveras le rideau'
And he is not was not here
But might have been:
A single gent in an en-
Suite with Matisse-like
Windows open to the sunlight:
It passed for two short decades
Over his square head,
Passed over and always
Jogged a mild '*déclic*'
That left him groping
In his memory of furnished rooms

– Koblenz Berlin Stockholm –
For shadows of perfume,
The *'frollement'* of Annie's hair.
Just movement really,
Sun shines recalling
An unceasing European shuttle,
The shape of all his journeys
Not their content.

I have a memory he would like
From the same blue room
He might have lodged in:
When from my bed
I turn my head towards
The estuary of little islands
In the loch, the rippling
Water's magnified by bevels
In the skinny window pane.
Cal Mac wobbles,
Bulging through bubbles in the glass:

Unsteady wake, awake
In the passing waves
Nozing for a line
Through my hour-glass pane.

I look again and this time
The window's inverted telescope
Shows me hillocks on the mull
Across the firth are fauve
With yellow gorse and broom
'Du rouge au vert tout le jaune se meurt'
And down on Fire Island Beach
Beneath the same sun Guillaume's
Lobbed across the kyle Frank wavers
In the sand too full of bourbon
To entirely catch its words:
Pollock, Patsy, Kline and Motherwell,
Madrid, Paris, Oscar Salvador and
Warren, marks among the falling
Grains – sun-dew – names
In poems Apollinaire made possible
And musical yes Frank the broken

Lines of barbecue sticks trace
Stories through the cottages of dunes
Until a buggy's headlights make a bee-
Line for you just as shrapnel did
For Guillaume.

'La fenêtre s'ouvre comme une orange'
I peel back the curtains
To the window bubbles
Streaming their oysterish
Juice 'Soleil cou coupé'

Ode tae Borborygmusses

eftir Valery Larbaud

Rift n' pump! Rift n' pump!
Deep curmurrin uv yer tummy an yer trollie-bags,
Girnin, fidgety flesh,
Voices, unstoppable whispery organs,
Wee yelps, the only patter 'at doesny lee,
An which persists even a bit eftir ye've popped yer veritable
　　clogs…

Doll, time n' again wi huv taen a wee brek fae oor
　　rumpy-pumpy
Tae listen tae the sang o oor ain intimmers;
Ach but it said it all – interminably sometimes –
While we tried oor level best no tae get thi kinks!
Up it cam fae deep doon,
Daft an ringin,
Louder an aw oor houghmagandy,
Mair unexpectit, mair inexorable, mair sairious –
Och the inevitable sang o thi oesophagus!
– stifled glug glug o a wee refreshment
the plop gloop plop o thi oary boats
plyin the pond i Queen's Park –
Christ but if it isny thi maist mysterious hingmygig
Ah'll niver again be able tae deny;
Sweet Mary an Joseph if it isny thi verra last wurd ah'll utter
When, still warm, ah'll be thi puir soul at soils the soil: a final
　　'Gardez-lou!'

Glossary

curmurrin – a rumbling noise; *trollie-bags* – entrails; *pop yer clogs* – die; *rumpy-pumpy* –
sex; *intimmers* – insides; *get thi kinks* – giggle uncontrollaby; *ringin* – imperious;
houghmagandy – sex; *hingmygig* – thingumygig.

A Hen Hop for Norman McLaren

In Sam Tata's 'cup of tea portrait of McLaren'
You're definitely cocked:
One eyebrow up, sniffing
Dissent, a nascent idea,
Sipping slantily…

And in 'McLaren, Cuba, 1962'
You're pure raunch:
Legs akimbo, ready to shoot
An unseen model from that side –
Aways smile and cloney moustache.

And in 'McLaren, Paris, 1950'
En route to Canada from China,
Educator you peers out,
Bespectacled, youngish,
Leaning a sparrow body
On a box camera called 'Hobie 17'.

But the stills don't reel you in.

You flicker back
On the silent film path
Of a 16mm Steenbeck
To Glasgow School of Art:
A symphony on the ciné-kodak special:
'Camera Makes Whoopee'.

In 'Seven Till Five'
You made Mackintosh's old swing doors
Blues in and out milk drinking students
With bad teeth, a rush of lips and life
Classes, cleaners' palettes, bells of pails,
Of steps, pollen dusted shepherd's pie.

But then cameras fell out of the frame:
In the intimate breeze of lit-up movement
You wanted contact: to touch up
The pellucid flesh of celluloid
And so 'etchcraft' began:

First de-emulsify, chisel the tip
Of a tiny knife, apply pen and India ink,
Thread the sound head of a moviola
And you've got a 'Boogie Doodle'
'Hen Hop', a 'Fiddle-de-dee'
'Begone Dull Care' to Oscar Peterson.

Just shapes in a jive,
No themes but in technique,
Although you couldn't help it
When the Klee-esque lines
Got human and the umbrella
Is a palm is a pineapple is a Slavic
Easter egg that hatches.

It was inevitable you'd end up
In a ballet, Norman,
Staggering a flux of dancers'
Entrechats, freezing then over-
Lapping frames to catch each iota
Of a plié.

How the light arm of 'Narcissus'
Makes a fan of longing!
You knew about that too:
The difficult, joyful exposure
Of strobing for the other in the same.

In a basement of the School of Art,
They sprinkle dust on celluloid
Because of you, sandpaper film
For smoky dusky, spray paint through
Chickenwire, hair nets and lace.

Take this comb then, this
Toothbrush, this cock-ring, these
Gear wheels, ball-bearings of words
And stroke, impress your silhouette
Upon the Glasgow light.

Customs

Customs vary: Rapunzel always
Sleeps on planes like this, slumped
Forward, waterfall of hair
Stepped over by a steward

As my gaze climbs it to the Prince
Beside her. Tenderly he pretends
To read a book quite stomached
By her beauty, portholed

Sunsets nesting on her crown.
The long-haul of my lover's
Snores fizzle up close by me.
We are dimmed. My spotlight

Aims optician's letters
At me through the glare:
Bug-like, icarian, they fall
Away and will not make a story.

This is patience. Half
Sleep fugs peripheral vision
And I am five again, intently
Glueing a balsa bi-plane

Until we touch the tarmac and it
Tenses like ryvita. We're stopped
At customs, two men travelling
Together. They ferret out the hidden

Freight of our pornography:
A Birthday card, a Christmas
Valentine. 'Sweetpart' to
'Sweetpart' and sillier names

Crease the fake gravitas
Of their faces. We haven't
Landed. My balsa plane dips,
Lurches over unexpected

Cliffs and as they gingerly
Remove each layer of sweaty
Socks, request receipts,
I ache for the reassuring

Touch of discreet fawn bark,
The ghost of tree rings,
The flight of your hand on mine.
Patience love. Wait

In the fearful patience
That is ours now
And forever. Soon the officer
Will close our case so the flight

Back may resume.

La Luna

In the Café Beaubourg,
Sunday honey drips
From Edmund White's pink
Jowls as he savours and emits

Gobbets of *The Sunday Times*
To a nephew who butters,
Listens and munches plangently.
The day is passing slowly.

A man shrugs and leaves,
Is offered more hair
By caricaturists on the cobbles
As he seeks 'La Luna'

In broad daylight. Rue Keller,
He notes a surveillance camera
Above the door, dry cleaners
Next to it, returns to his hotel

And waits for dark. Much later

He yawningly accepts free
Lube and condoms, relies
On someone else's poppers,
Encounters the fierce gaze

Of fifty-five cropped youths
With hairless pecs and pubes.
Then, to techno, the whole thing
Speeds up in a basement full

Of mock scaffolding, bricked-
Up alleys and just as arching
Thighs glimmer in the darkness
The clank of a bracelet

Reminds him of the spirit
Of the place. It surges
Through the hollow pipes:
A tiny jangling skeleton

That races in its dinky-toy
Up and down the maze of loops
And tubes, snapping
Its piranha teeth through

The spy-holes of loose screws.
Deflation, sick fear, short-
Circuit the hard-
Core dance and he goes

Home, jerks off slowly
To late-night porn cabled
On the adult channel.
The studs and twinkies finally

Dissolve into the freeze-
Frame of an emaciated smile
Resolving from the mist of static:
A smile that widens

As it whitens the screen's
Empty maw, the pristine grin
Of the Ex he left
Just before the end set in.

Ibiza 1985

Clad in a sheen of 'Factor 2',
Triceps clench: the Trierarch thrusts
Out, dips from the trireme's plunge-deck:
Six foot three of muscle mary
Dark as an eclipse.

A faint Phoenician breeze
Oils his back which butterflies through surf
Before he knees the waves
Towards the beach:
Es Cavallet awakes

As Punic Bes creates young men
Around him: they dart from parasols
In homage to his Perfect Definition,
Douche salty lips with Evian while Ray Bans
Flash small lizard tongues of light
He coasts along at full tilt for the bar.

His boys return to ritual tans,
Prize twigs and butts from toes,
Throb to the techno trance of Pitusian
Crickets rasping in the dunes.

These men ignore an August snow
Which smothers more of them each year:
White bodies dotting sunbeds
Ferried by lifeguards for them
Across the soft Ibizan sand,

Whiter, as the white corpuscles
Drop, than ash in cinerary urns
Of the neighbourhood necropolis
Where Carthage sent her dead.
Tonight they dance at the disco
Amphora and the joke
Will soon be lost on them.

The beach pours from its scorching jar:
Sombrillas flame a frieze of rainbow
Coloured flags about its neck.
Beneath their shade, rows of boys
Await discovery, robbery, the bland
Photography of future times,
Finger treasures that will not burn:
Cornaline scarab, jasper amulet,
Ostrich eggs and unguent pots,
Washed bones, lamps for the dark.

Wall

PYRAMUS: *O, kiss me through the hole of this vile wall!*
THISBE: *I kiss the wall's hole, not your lips at all.*
Shakespeare, *A Midsummer Night's Dream*

Look at the wall, the sweet and lovely
Wall we carry with us in public places.
Even in meadows when we rest it
For a second on muscular buttercups,

Its tinyness glimpsed from the distances
Of outer galaxies is not as small
As the monstrous little voice
I use to whisper to you through its chink.

And in the streets of Glasgow
Where we set it down despite the looks
To share affection over *lattes* and Versace suits
We can hear the awkward avalanche

Of lime and mortar evolve within its frame
As we kneel down and seek out
Chink and speak our cherry words
Knit up in hair and stone.

Even here on Pearblossom Highway
Or Garrowby Hill where you can barely
See it for the Hockney colours
And sentimentalists mistake it for a rainbow

It is a wall that bears our mottoes of restraint.
And in the Japanese storyboard
Of Chris and Don's Malibu interior
Where even the wicker chairs are clearly

Gay, at ease with their own maturity,
Wall balances between the pockets
Of our cargo pants as we meander through,
Fearful of prat-fall, putty on the pinewood floor.

Some say Chink offers us the virtue
Of cubist perspective: the silk forest
Of your ear-lobe's blonde still-baby
Hairs. Polaroided and collaged

In a cakewalk of mismatching
Edges, our groins grow a wall.
Exciting textures are described
But no one ever asks us what it weighs.

Others tell us to ignore it, drape
Our bodies in a magnetic web
Of invisible embraces, a shimmering
Virtual cloth of Proustian complexity

Beyond the deconstructive powers
Of Peter Quince. We touch our asses
Heads like caps, pick up our wall
And walk. True, Chink's lynx eye

Offers us a precious parsimony
Of moments: the time the slits
Of our lapels smiled to fill the whole
Of that slim orifice, the time

Your pinkie stroked a whisker
Of my orange tawny beard,
My purple-in-grain beard,
My French crown-colour beard!

And no one noticed!
But those who see our wall and label it
Know about its chink as well,
The slight pucker of its lips

Which taste of cold, chipped tile,
Name it only for the fuck hole
Of Bully Bottom's rude mechanicals.
Everywhere we turn we find out

Moonshine. Smash wall!
Smash the person of wall
And the person
Of pure moonshine!

Balance. Poise. The gentle pirouette of Janus on the doorstep, his moment before invocation, convocation. Not indecision but that flexing hesitation where thought gathers and matures before words marshal sense into fruitful law. Hail to the thresholds of a Scottish Parliament! Neither *of* chambers, ante-rooms or corridors. Nor without them. But slight borders, unnoticed margins, hems to the ermine, light-filled spaces of debate. No thresholds barred! No threshold; yet present everywhere, anytime; shape of shadow cast through window, stone's lip of cement and mortar, the frame of someone's glasses glinting reminding you of frailty and vision. Threshold is amendment. Modest footnote on the door-stane, drumming of fingers on tables where just forms of words are sought. In Scots it's *threshwart, thrashel, lintel* and *door-sole*. And in the door's soul the days with all their differences and contradictions are visible. And they are held in the palm of *door-sole* and communicate, commune with all within doors that is common, the same as we seem we've always been, folk from this airt. The thresholds of a Scottish Parliament are palms that sign its body with the timbre of heel and instep, discreet life-line, pinkie and little toe. They sign the etymology of 'threshold', our foreign roots, reminding us that once here was there, that once some of us were them, saying, signing: do not slam the door on *threscwald, threxwold*; from *thresc-an ferire*, and *wald liguum*, i.e. the wood which one strikes with one's feet at entering or going out of a house. Do not slam the door on South Germany's *trooskel*, Denmark's *taerskel* or Iceland's *throskulld-ur*. Within the door-stane smeddum of the thresholds of a Scottish Parliament the delicate hyphens pivot, rocking its peoples inwards, outwards to the translated melodies of Carmichael's blessing:

> Grace of the threshold be thine
> Grace of floor and ceiling
> From site to stay
> From beam to wall,
> From balk to roof-tree,
> From found to summit
> Found and summit

Here is the morning-evening blessing of the house, the Gaelic-Scots-English, each inflecting each, each turned to each. Strike hard upon this wood. Knock upon the wood of the great boat shapes an architect has placed above our heads in echo of the sailing thresholds of our Parliament.

Saltires

for Richard Price

Where in red is the true red? The original prime colour to which all *other reds aspire?*
Derek Jarman, *Chroma*

At school I'd hair so red my Australian
English teacher called me '*Bluey*!'
And it's that queer logic
Helps you to appreciate
Petitioners of our Parliament
Who wish to regulate
The Saltire's shade of blue.

They look up to crenellated bits:
The pretended family flutter
Of white on blue flagging up
A cloudy sky, aspiring
To the true Idea of ultra-marine,
That Virgin Queen
Who staked out auld St Andro
In his game of naughts and crosses.

They want the stalled rap
Of an Yves Klein blue
To brand headquarters with,
A potato-printed flag
To pattern tiling of the best kept
Public loos in Scotland.

As for that white *piste*:
It leads through miles of boring
Dark-blue firs to more blue firs
Primed for logging: a dominie
Moistens his pencil tip,
Sharpens his bark

And the chalk dust rises
To white-out discrepancies,
A channel of alban cemeteries
Criss-crossing blue estates.

What should we fly
From Scotland's drizzlements?

A piece of blue oatcake
Found on the Field of Culloden
And blue grapeshot from the same battle

A blue pocket book worked by Flora
MacDonald and a blue box
Made of the pulley of the Scottish
Maiden (a form of guillotine)

A blue quaich made from Queen Mary's yew

A blue lock of Lord
Nelson's hair (sent by Lady
Hamilton to the Prince Regent
Who personally gave it to Mrs
MacMahon who gave it to Mr
Magrath who presented it to Sir
Walter in 1817)

Blue lines
On Burns' tumbler cut
With a blue diamond by the Poet.

Blue? But we live in a whole
Geography of colour:
Antwerp blue, Mars violet
Or the 'little pans of watercolour'
We can dip into now and again,
Manganese blue or blue of the bugloss,
'Blue of the sage and winter hyacinth.'

Or no blue at all,
But the colours that hide
In our Colours, in the creases
Created by snell East-coast gusts
Up on a jaunt from the Forth.

What rainbows bend
Through the prisms that tip
From blue furls
Before they re-jink into white,
The grooves of our national straits?

And even those Grooves
Can groove in the wind
That stipples the sun in a silver
Fizzle across the blues
Of Flowerdale Bay.

Its blues are waters
That simply purr
Around an evening pier
Before the pastel pink
Flag of The Bruce
Sashays the sky to Skye.

Rough twists graze
The soft downed thighs:
A rope held stiff
Between his legs,
He fingers the smooth brown
Glans that ties it off.

Soon a gym teacher will bark
And the boy flail
About the floor
While others mostly squirm and
Thrust up, up, up:
He would swing out now

But the backs of his legs
Are slammed against a wall-bar
Forcing a head-stand,
Penalty for failing flailing

He should swing not take it
Quite so much to heart!
He's magic after all,
All boys know it: poofs can fly!

But in the chemistry lab
No one wants to partner him
Because his explosions
Make the test-tubes cum.

He would swing out
With Donald's new-born biceps,
Jungle-gym the pommel horse
And vault up to where Mike's
Soft and tiny velvet prick
Peeps out his rucked-up pants
To wink at him.

He would swing out
At the chequered ball
But they pick him last
Because he always kicks
At invisible goals a foot
To the left of the real one.

He would swing out now
But they steal the broomstick
Of his bag and ride it
'Out of Bounds'
And then they swing for him.

He would swing out now
And here in the midnight gym
– the masters and the boys coiled in their dreams –
Are the nudging ropes
And the bench:

Twelve pendulums of hemp
To thrash the air with
He waits an age
For them to be still again
He could swing out now

Or climb
Up up up.

The Barrier

But good-night! – God bless-you!
 The stillness of true loss:
Sterne says, that is equal to a kiss:
 it wakes with him. It is
yet I would rather give you the kiss
 the moment before full
into the bargain, glowing with
 consciousness and the
gratitude to heaven, and affection
 moment after. It is the
to you. I like the word affection,
 utter stillness of pure
because it signifies something
 loss held like a sweet
habitual; and we are soon to
 contemplated face in the
meet, to try whether we have
 bed of love, held for a
mind enough to keep our
 second before movement,
hearts warm. – Mary.
 before life. It is the descending
I will be at the barrier
 certainty that you are purely
a little after ten o'clock
 alone forever and that no one,
tomorrow.
 no one can ever touch that

loneliness and loss.
Mary Wollstonecraft

Turned away from me,

       I read the sadness of pure
       loss as it floods his face –
       although I cannot see it.
       The still terror and yet
       the acceptance of that
       terror in the silent morning
       bed before light and
       movement. The impossibility
       of fully naming it, the im-
       possibility of being in it.

Bed

The moment the light goes out,
He sleeps: a gift from the dark.
There is the small chime
Of the moon on the wall,
The deep freeze digesting
In the kitchen. He floats
From head to toe on the buzz
Of his snore, dreaming the calm
Glide of a Jasper ski-lift,
The summer elk that trotted
Out of forest beneath our
Dangling feet. His arm
Crooks the violin of my head.
I elbow him away intent on
Sleep but suddenly unpegged
By a gust of dreams we roll
Together in the hot hole
Of his mum's old bed,
Dribbling on the pillows.
Waking, he has me in an
Arm-lock, our legs a single
Rope of flesh, my ear-lobe
Tickled by his breath. I reach
Behind me and shove my hand
Between his thighs. He stretches,
Opening briefly like a centre-
Fold, a light smile of welcome
On his lips. But more than this
Is the scrape of the two-o'clock
Beetle, the nip of a dust-mite,
My scratch: my love disturbed
By me, awake but patient
In the dark.

DES LITS DE GUIBERT
(Of Guibert's Beds)

It has been claimed by the most erudite authorities that these pages were found among the papers of the late Hervé Guibert, the French novelist, after his death from AIDS-related illnesses in 1991. Part 2 purports to be written by an acquaintance of Guibert, 'le professeur David Kinloch'.

Translated from the French by David Kinloch.

1

I had discharged myself from my hospital deathbed (in the Pavillon Falguière to be precise), despite the direst warnings of le docteur Chandi, and had boarded a plane en route for Glasgow in Scotland and then, several hours later, a small eight seater bound for the Isle of Lewis, the most northerly of the Outer Hebrides, as instructed by a minor acquaintance – cruised briefly in Le Mic-Mac Man I think in 1988 – a young, or rather younger, Scottish poet and academic, David Kinloch, who, on several occasions during the months of my final decline had offered me the inviting prospect of a short stay with him in that land of mist and romance (believing, of course, that I would never make the trip), our temporary abode being the Carrick View Guest House – proprietor J. MacLeod – not far from the standing stones of Callanish of some five thousand years antiquity.

Such a trip was quite in keeping with the restless image I had cultivated for years, years which had seen trips to Rome, Rio, Hamburg, Moscow, Rome again, always in fact returning to Rome whose every stone oozes art quite unlike these Scottish stones which could, and probably will, resemble my tombstone (swollen to gigantic proportions and conveniently fauve in its ruggedness) were I to choose to have one – which I won't, of course.

This journey, however, was a little different from the others, most of which had been tantalising quests in search of paintings and other 'objets d'art' some of which I suspected – with a frisson only deadmen reared on placebos can know – might be fakes. I had now reached the stage of my year-long death at which each and every bedroom I entered might contain my deathbed. It was a kind of dormitory Russian roulette: each chamber appeared empty at first until I caught sight of the death-head grinning back at me from the hotel mirror. After a month or so of this, I began to see that these bedrooms and hospital wards had to form part of the process I had begun some three

57

years earlier, partly recorded in my masterpiece *A l'ami qui ne m'a pas sauvé la vie.* This work and others had been crucial steps in the ongoing process of outwitting and domesticating the HIV virus, ceaselessly replicating itself in my blood, by producing – and the emphasis was very much on the act itself of writing, the replicating of the replicating in fact – descriptions and analyses of my final years and months, making the illnesses visited on me by this odd parasite an integral and in a sense *loved* part of my being. This was a joyous morbidity indeed, not dissimilar in some respects to the 'joyous anger' Almaviva detects in Figaro. Just as I had had to inject the unutterable queerness of the virus into my pen so I needed to make these beds, where I spent more and more of my time, my familiar, no matter how strange they might at first appear; the stranger the better in fact, for thanks to the virtuosity of that very same pen I would then be able to die in one with a smidgen of equanimity.

I began to roam – it is difficult to shake off the word – both the globe and its libraries in search of bedrooms as inimical as possible to the *petit pedé parisien* I had become in my innermost being. The libraries were mere relaxation, dilettantism, yet there I made the pleasing discovery that the clinics from which I was attempting to escape derive their name from the ancient Greek, *kline,* meaning bed. The *Nationale* afforded me beds in folio: of Assurbanipal, of Niniveh, of Solomon's cedar wood temple. The *Mazarine* brought me to the *Tipi* of the Pawnees and in Arabia I lay on baldaquins, divans, sofas, tabourets, all *choses jetées à terre.*

The voyage to Lewis was a most earnest attempt to meet the *other* head on: I imagined – because I had been told by that false friend, that epitome of academic fakery, *le professeur Kinloch* – brochs, blackhouses, thatch, byres. Imagine my dismay, my contempt therefore, when the simple B and B, barely roofed against the elements, turned out to be an establishment with *Taste of Scotland* florets, double glazing, a pink and blue bedroom of ineffable comfort – the kind I insisted on calling *le confort anglais* to spite my host – perfidious Albion!

In the evening I retired to my *cubiculum* with Dibie's *Ethnologie de la chambre à coucher* and there, in that stifling Hebridean snug, sunk into a fitful sleep, wrapped – or so I dreamt – in a convertible fishing net of the type which doubled as a hammock and gauzy protection against the mosquitoes that used to suck on the primitive ancestors of my Scottish hosts five thousand years ago.

2

Tiny black pellets from the tight arses of sheep, the acrid, candied reek of peat smoke, shades of grey dappling to the west like the underbelly of Johnson's baby cotton wool, Lewis littering these northern seas, eventually all this seduced his sweet telephone voice and Hervé Guibert promised to come with me to the Outer Hebrides: 'Yes!' he had yelped. 'Nothing could be queerer! I'll come.'

Yet he was so far gone in his various illnesses by the time he reached me that when he stepped gingerly from the plane I could see no difference. Guibert and Lewis were one as the wind rushed into the cavern of his MacIntosh like a druid to the protective hug of a standing stone. The flight from Glasgow was full and as the passengers packed into the tiny, corrugated hut that served as terminal building they shifted uneasily aside as Guibert struggled through them to collect his case. You only had to look at him to see what was wrong. Somehow they couldn't perceive that all they had before them was a bit of the land itself, dark and barren like the peat-bogs, a hooded walking stone collecting a battered case from the trolley. Soon it would be different though. In a month or two. When he would be machair, rivulets of rain on the tarmac.

With his delicate French accent he would try to pronounce the Gaelic names of the villages we drove through but he could never get to the end and his voice would sink to a whisper at the crossroads of a particularly difficult cluster of vowels. I could be of little help to him and eventually he gave up, his eyes as vacant as the white diamond boards that marked passing places on the single-track roads. Only once did he leap to attention, grabbing the map from his knee, forcing me to stop the car so that he could confirm the English version of *Barabhas*. This place, pronounced Barvas, which seemed to bear the name of the thief ransomed by the crowd in preference to Jesus, was a self-inflicted village of the plain, with ramshackle cottages, rusting buses in peat-bogs, dreich as the first Sunday after creation. It was dominated by a huge barnlike church with a car-park as big as a supermarket. Light the colour of sperm poured through tall, thin windows from the other side of the building. We could see a simple wooden stair and nothing else. At this point, Guibert said he 'would like to walk a little in Barabhas'. I pointed out that there were wonderful beaches in close proximity 'with air that will be wholesome to your lungs'. But he was quite insistent. As, indeed, was a sheep which butted him so hard in the thigh on his descent from the car that we both feared broken bones. Guibert failed to see the humour in the situation and thereafter glared at every docile creature munching its way along our road.

A look of deep foreboding came over his face as we reached the sands of Uig. I paid no attention, however, and he walked quietly with me down onto the beach. We buffeted our way right to the centre of the vast expanse, skirting rafts of water abandoned by the tide, caught in the streams of skating sand that swerved around our ankles. 'On dirait Maspalomas,' Guibert murmured. For a moment he bent down and I noticed that here the wind had slashed with such ferocity that it looked as if thousands of bullets had strafed across the beach. Little broken shells, slivers of razor blades, white and blue, had caught there in the helter-skelter from the sea and perched like flags or hats on the tiny peaks of sand.

But Guibert wanted to press on to Rodel and the Church of St Clement. It was typical of him that he should make a bee-line for the one place on the island where art surely triumphed over nature. Soon we were standing in the simple twelfth-century church before the tomb of Alastair Crotach or Alexander VII of Harris to give him his proper title. The guidebook informed Guibert that this was the most impressive item of medieval art in the Western Isles but he needed little telling. Alastair's armour-clad effigy lay carved in black stone but above him an arched canopy of chiselled panels depicted both his fleshly and actual heavenly lives.

Just at this moment, sun from a window in the north transept moved through the church and stole slowly across the whole tomb, making the quartz crystals in the schist sparkle. Panel by sunlit panel, the tomb broke into life: the sails of a stone galley billowed briefly in the glitter and a smile broke like a wave across hunting stagmen. A devil chatted to St Michael as they weighed the peat-slabs that were Alastair's sins. Guibert was silent for a while, then smiled and said that he loved the galley, the castle and the stag hunt and thanked me for bringing him here.

His interest brightened considerably, however, when I explained from the guidebook that the sarcophagus was almost certainly empty, the remains having been removed to an anonymous burial ground in the cemetery when news had come of an impending invasion. Alastair's oval helmet and sword contained no bones, no steel, no residual DNA. He was a shell, a fake and the spirit of St Clement's was just the devious Hebridean light. As we left, Guibert remarked that Alastair Crotacht must have been a tyrant and patron worth knowing.

3   Guibert's Rodel Poem

The road that brings you me
is silverweed and tormentil
bird's-foot trefoil and all
the machair flowers.

I give the road that brings
you me, out-crop, windows
infilled with six-spokes, the grave-
slab of the Chamberlain of Harris.

The road that brings you me
baptises with font,
with apse and human heads
wrought in freestone,
badly weathered gneiss.

The road that brings me
places you gently in pediment
and recess, thing that tilled
lazy-beds, creature of
centaury, eyebright and thyme.

The road that brings me
grants you eyes of schist,
a body of amphibolite,
carved galleys and castles
to swim upon your chest.

Royal ferns glitter about
the brow of Black Guibert,
lying in his sequinned quartz.

4   Barabbas

I have brought with me, from Paris to Lewis, nothing but my recur-
ring dream of the nightingale floor – *le plancher des rossignols* – more
melodious in French than in English but in fact created by timorous
Japanese to warn them of the shapes the darkness takes. Singing
parquet! It sparkles with birdsong in my sleep, my highland futon
pierced by the local piping of sandpiper and dipper, waking me to the
shadows of Gaelic samourai and hatamoto who steal with Mrs
MacLeod about my floral walls. *Rossignol! Rossignol!* Each cry bursts a
T-cell. Count! Count! Each note is a footstep in my blood, each enemy
that comes has a different mask and name. I count the multitudinous
names of beds: *lectuli, triclinium, lectisterniacor, lectica* sheeply somersault
beneath my lids. Which one will I die in? Towards dawn, I am the
queen-pin in a sickly 'lever de la reine' assisted with my regalia by vying

buddies. *Rossignol!* And this nightingale landscape is like the day where Lewis is creole, impure: breaker, machair, peat-bog, rock, knoll, scrub, burnt heather, a scribbled brown, a scribbled black, a dash of blue, a pinch of green and slate, interminable grey and cloud turn through my double vision with the voracity of unceasing Z-bends. Stop, go, stop, go! The nightingale passing places!

Two kilometres past Barabhas now. At least its name is certain, no joke intended. But what of *Breascleit, Carlabhagh, Siabost, Gearraidh na-Aibhne?* Such shifting sand is all too familiar to me; I will write its declivities up: I saw a river of blood this morning and would not ascribe it all to peat. Yet I ache for the regularity of a solid *immeuble* by Haussman, bevelled brick and the reliable filigree of an unused verandah. The isle is full of voices. What hubris to think they could be changed into the being of a little Frenchman! *Rossignol!* Off with these Gaelic etymologies! Bring me at last to the home-rooted bed of Ulysses, fast in the heart of two kissing olive trees built about by walls and entered by a door. Finer than the beds of Circe, Calypso, Nausicaa, the retching bed of the Tarbert ferry, the bed of the shipwrecked sand. Nightingale beds that cry beware! or fake! I would swing my feet from the hammock of my B and B and plant them firmly on the ground but, looking down, this is – what? – floor, rug, thick pile, parquet, the slight song of a dreaming bird. Like the waking Eskimos, I move slowly, with infinite care, lest the hundred souls that lodge in my body's articulations be bruised, put out of joint. Snipe cry past the window from the loch. Here is *adek,* soul of life, whose seat is at the base of my neck and soul of sleep couched beneath my diaphragm. Gently. Doucement. Sometimes I wonder if he's laughing at me, that nightingale. What would he laugh at? What?! My life, my closing days, this mulatto island, these Gaelic words are like the Inuit's floor of ice, clear for several metres but then, in sleep, we hear his tongue chirping two thousand different names for it. I lie in Mrs MacLeod's thrice recommended establishment and am a dictionary of ice, three thousand feet deep in places. Listen. I crave plain ice but here there is *svell,* in modern usage 'ice with solid ground beneath'. Above the lintel of her door there is *iss,* ice on water, *svell-ottr,* water swollen with lumps of ice. At Rodel that morning, amidst the pain and beauty of my many cancers, my rossignols, the sunny, empty tomb of Alastair laid upon me *handar svell, the ice of the hand,* gold and *sars dreya, fetla svell, wound-ice, weapons.* I gaze on the standing stones of Callanish, five thousand years of stone and beg for *klaki, hard-frozen ground.* They answer back: *koma e-m a kaldan klaka,* the phrase, *to put one on a cold ice-field, to bring one into distress.* One stone is frozen turf, *klaka-torf,* one stone is *klaka-hogg,* crowbar to break the frozen ground, my friend the gravedigger.

UN TOUR D'ECOSSE

The creation of a cycle tour of France is part of the fall out from the Dreyfus Affair, the conflict which, at the end of the nineteenth century, tore France as if it were an antagonistic couple into two mutually mistrustful halves (...): some rightly defended the Captain's innocence at the risk of casting aspersion on the illusory ideal of national purity; others subscribed to the spotless national ideal and advocated the traitrous Captain's erasure; the whole affair set alight a wave of unprecedented anti-semitism.

Following a similar pattern, the invention of the Tour was encouraged by the bitter but stimulating duel which opposed Pierre Giffard, director of the paper Le Vélo *and Henri Desgranges who reproached his rival not with supporting Captain Dreyfus but with having done so in the columns of a sporting journal, which, in his opinion, would simply make the painful conflict worse instead of distracting from it.*

Desgranges (...) replaced the sterile shapes of divisiveness with those of the Tour (...) an opening inscribed upon France's surface written by the chain of racers which, in revealing the country's wonderful diversity, shaped itself in relation to the victor, as a sentence does about its principal clause.

Translated from Josée Lapeyrère's *Comment faire le Tour*

Pédale: etym: 1 étrier. 2 sodomie/ite. De l'expression: faire de la pédale, courber les reins. Descendre par la pédale: abandonner lachement une course. Quitter les pédales: être décontenancé, perdre son assurance. Perdre les pédales: déraisonner. Lacher les pédales: penser à une intrigue amoureuse.

Dictionnaire historique des argots français

Lorca on Morar

Lorca:

'Areesaig', 'Morrarr…'
the beach stands up
in little whirlwinds of ash
in my Hispanic mouth,

the dunes become chintz
statues of white sand,
poodles with griffon beaks.

Mannerism of stranded sea-horses!
Salute a small poet
murdered for being red and gay.

All the spaces of Scotland
disclose me without warning,
beam me down from whatever limbo
buries in the olive prose of death.

Now: this purgatory,
ghost country whose name
never crossed my lips.

Morar, morire, muerte:
my very element
from which I hail Atlantic
breakers and you
'beautiful old Walt Whitman'.

Camerado

Whitman:

Camerado Federico!
I stride and stroll on Paumanock,
Immortelle of Manahatta,
I stoop to listen to the leopard froth
As it gazelles the beach like fizzing bicycles.
I straddle it, I beard and balance
Its promenade of handlebars, kneel to pluck
The tart-sweet daisies flowering in its rust
And – there! – unfurling in its clare-
Obscure accept your butterfly of song.

Great gorgeous creature of gamboge and black!
I pin you to my beard, I fasten you
Upon the snowfield of my whiskers.
Shrouded bard of another land
Here is the exquisite flexible door of the sea.
Let us suffer its changes together.
Race with me! Let me bless and buff you!
The spokes and paddles of our fresh entente
Arise and your contemptible dreams recede.

Greengown

Lorca:

How hard 'greengown' tries! How hard it tries to become more than a word in a dictionary. How hard it seeks for a shuttling hyphen that will green out the dark columns without a backward glance towards the gown of swirling faces. Each time it walks towards me, it looks back. I hear meadow song in a cave, an angel-gale of night, catch the glimmer of half-moon lemon rinds stitched at cuff and collar. My gown of grenadine velvet coming, coming to inhabit me! But then a wave gloops, the green instep fills with water. Why should this foreign word, found in a dictionary, so attract me? 'Greengown: the loss of virginity in open air; sod, turf on a grave.' Look at the pale blue-fleshed worms balancing tiny leaves on the tongues of their white jelly snouts. They push their heads through green ruffs of chlorophyll and nudge with infinite slowness into the obscure meaning of their being. Together we wait for the gravedigger, wait in this lychgate earth, our bodies raped by the sky. After an eternity a man will come and fold me into this Scottish word. He will dishevel Spanish earth from my shoulders, with his heel force me deep, soil me with his strong foreign hands. With the worms I will crawl into the pure pain of this nation's white thigh bone and a space will get up and walk. Greengown will be Lorca and Lorca greengown. How hard Lorca tries to become Scotland. How hard Scotland tries to be the earth's timeless doors which revolve the blush of fruit like bicycle wheels. How hard Scotland tries to become el cri cri de las margaritas: daisy cry daisy cry at the broken chain of the alphabet.

Scotland

to Robert Crawford

Mountainbike country, miniature monocoque
Of machair and big air; from above
Your cities are velociraptors, twister spools
Of spinergy; yellow jersey country snugged
Finger-tight, a stutter-bump off Europe.

Don Quixote of the derailleurs,
You magnetize the towns and villages
To the maypole of their TV sets;
It birls them on a Tour d'Ecosse,
Encompassing the oddity of every airt and pairt;

Kelso skids on Elgin's peewit bell,
Coll chimichangas up the Butt of Lewis
Dundee breakdances on its bars,
Grins up at the basket of your tiny
Wildflower face: primula scotica,

Kama Sutra of freewheeling petals:
Old-tech hip-hop, cog-country, nipple
Nation. To love you is just to race you,
Reel serious dirt time through a marram
Grass of spokes: cinemas of the real.

Sauchehall Street Orange

The journalists – cameras, bags bristling with mikes, little notebooks – wait for the Spanish champion.

Josée Lapeyrère, *Comment faire le Tour*

Lorca:

Sauchiehall Street is the street of weeping willows. All gone! Nor are there orchards for which the medieval city was once famous. Imagine a Glasgow of orange and lemon trees! Orange. Even the way the word is pronounced here misses its succulence. The hard, bitter zest of 'naranja' which deliquesces into froth of air, or the orotund 'jouissance' of the word in French, is flattened, clipped, emphasis on the 'or' offering choice which does not seem to exist for many here and the French angel in 'ange' floats silently like snow over its unpronounced syllables and vowels. I place 'naranja' in Sauchiehall Street and convoque the angel of choice to crown it like a fairy. Grasp a lith of its firm rind and dance round it. Maypole of the orange tree! It is not May yet. Perhaps you will come in May. Will we dance together?

Gnarly Downhills

Whitman:

Come! Let's sprint the gnarly down-
Hill fire road of the sea!
Our ferries transmigrate to bicycles!
My feet shod in shaker shoes of fog
Shed clogs of Massachusetts barks.
Strip down to match your bracing
Aluminium frame. Twist shifter!
Reveal your turbo-grip as I disclose mine:
The pine bateau of my saddle,
Your bell of linden barque, behold
My spruce dahabiyah mud-guards,
Your cedar ketch handlebars!
Let's ovalize, double-butt,
Oversize to ensure extreme stress
Disbursement. You'll feel the better
Of my suspended otter!
Here are our wheels of hickorie galleon,
The hornbeam funny of my ass,
The sassafras ferry of your crotch.
They nestle in the just-felt
Breezes of my overtaking.
Place this simplelock head strap
And nine full flow cooling vents
About your head. It wreathes
Torque sensitive systems
With its infinite burns.
The race is on, so float
And toss with me, strain
On your sharp Spanish waist
And surf the bent ocean
With the simplicity of a single pivot.

Rind

O cycle of the lemon rind
Peel back your silver thighs
Along the yellow coastal roads;
At the seventh circle,
Lean into the sun's hot core,
Be mule saddle,
Strike from the crossbar
Like a stubborn branch
And let the green pith
Ring its bitter bell.

Grass

Whitman:

Federico foofoo! Freckleless, shaven and almond-eyed. Have you noticed the grass which floats in the stagnant waters of harbours or the unexpected hair of bright grass encountered in the salt transparent greenshine of the open sea? I see how it curls suddenly in the water, a grass of silver fish, a tiny cutting through which your face peeps out beckoning me to cabs and coupés of the waves. Why do your commas become so gracefully seahorse eyebrows, the plucky chug of little shad-boats? I would pass through the paper ocean to you if I could, just one simple letter and your sorrow would drown in the flambeau of my hope. Oh barouches of troughs, open wide for the tilth of me! Let my fat splash kindle the cold type into flesh! At five in the afternoon your ode jinked round the Battery, fluttered through sloops and skiffs, the marvellously beautiful yachts, alighted for honey toddy on Staten Island and then, as if pouring the whole sea from the palms of your wings, called out to me to save you. I hear your notes, I hear your call, I hear, I come presently. But how do I interpret that spiritual insect voice? A shower of colour sends overhand and underhand and overhand, that lightly shedding of palms and roofs of palms we played as children, stacking our playful angers like playing cards: thus your voice in the sea, your voice and the sea at the harbour wall: your entreaty slapping up to me. Heave'e yo stevedore! I put out for you as you put out for me! Rendezvous: the hot Atlantic currents, a gulf stream pedalling furious into Carradale, the palm-fringed Scottish villages.

Little Glasgow Ceilidh

¡ay, ay, ay, ay!
Toma este vals con la boca cerrada
　　　　　　Lorca, *'Paqueño vals vienés'*

Lorca:

Aye, aye, aye, aye!
Old penis poet,
Your grizzled scrotum
Droops upon my saddle
As you ride me up and down
The Scottish roads
With no respect for my discretion.

Aye, aye, aye, aye!
Little ceilidh of humiliation,
Full of reeling sergeants
That I don't know how to dash.

You'd out me
To the pigeons of George Square,
Loud spermicidal windbag,
You play these games
With tartan names
And defunct patois
But what will a Parliament do
For Scottish poofs?

Tiny ceilidh, minuscule ceilidh, angelic pin-head ceilidh
Of itself, of death, of usquebaugh,
That dips its sporran in the sea.

If we dared, we'd speak about
MPs of 'unfounded rumour'
Who in time of civil war
Just shoot you up the arse.

Or picture William of Dumfries
Who dials his lover
From a red box in a smudge of weather:
Go ahead please, you're through
To the next stage of the disease.

Aye, aye, aye, aye!
Little ceilidh of blood puddings
And pudding featured biggots.

This author can't download
Our sensibilities, then re-mix
Us to his taste and race us
Like a tandem mountain-bike
About the bonny, bloody heather.

To the natives, we are as all should be
Who cannot choose the way they are
And are *this* way: American Uncles,
Pure fiction or a foreign plague,
Not Scottish. Nut. Not ever.

Aye, aye, aye, aye!
Little ceilidh of fedupness,
Take this 'I will always hate you' ceilidh.

Old penis beard,
I deflate your tyres and watch you
Double somersault the machair!
Walt Whitman go home.
Your pen is never feminine.
Leave me to my obliquity
And aim your frankness more directly.

Braveheart

Preceded by his manager, he surges out of the dim interior of the hotel, light-footed, graceful, a clear far-away look in his eyes…

Comment faire le Tour

O Mel! Mel of the hair extenders! Braveheart!
O Mad Mac Mel! It is I,
Walt, Walt Whitman, who salutes you.
When I heard at the close of the day
That your heroic film of the Wallace
Would premiere in Stirling, I floated

From Mount Florida, high above Glasgow, floated
From the residence of my comrade Kinloch, a brave heart
Like you, I crossed the hummock-land of Shotts as Wallace
Did on leaving Elderslie, I
Sped through that dun-coloured upland (beside the great M8) that day
To celebrate your epic but most of all to be with you

O Mel! But also to petition you,
Dark singer of Democracy, you who floated
Like a Moses through Scottish bogs, waiting for the day
To release your noble, simple people, their brave brave heart
Clasped in an English vice. O Mel, I
Confuse you, mix you in my mind with Wallace.

And who could blame me? For you and Wallace
Commingle in my scented breast, you
Two and I, comrades all, shooting the film of liberty I
Crave above all else, I crave and lost as my successors floated
Back up stream to a land of villanelles and sonnets. Bravehearts!
Brave Walt! a bearded Ariel imprisoned in a bad sestina who would
                                                              this day

Be free again by your example, free today
To live today, to sing the love of comrades as Wallace
Did. He could not rhyme, his only beat the braveheart
Quad-pumping the eclectic plaid about his knees (What knees!). You
Saw him Mel, as clearly as I see you who floated
From Australia via Hollywood to this premiere. I

Name the perfumed guests as they arrive, I
Shake the manly hand of Jodie Foster, day
Dream as Christian Slater – he of the slow doe-eyes – floats
In. We sit transfixed as the credits of your Wallace
Roll but I have eyes alone for you,
Peach of a biceps – your musk white thighs – muncher of
                                    power-breakfasts, Braveheart!

Mel Wallace, Will Gibson, this day
Your barbaric yawp injects its braveheart
Into me. You and I floating and free.

Moulton-Mini

Childhood of the moulton-mini! Insanely blue poney with wheels! I led gangs of you about the 'Avenues', colonised 'triangles' of trees, made crazy war on tougher boys from vernacular districts of the south, received black'n'blue 'keekers', gravel of contempt, tearing love in my crotch. Apollonian boys of Daisy Street! Indian Summer of '76! Little fable of exclamations! At some soulless interchange you turn into question-marks: the moulton-mini is an exercise bike static in a gym: Wheat Ridge, seven kilometres of digitised bends, dot-matrix mountains. A red light blinks and The Pacer is upon you: allez! Stand up in the pedals: odd flashing words overtake you: 'soul', 'wheat', 'Saturn' 'snowfields'. What I gasp instead: 'empty', 'adrift', 'ripped', 'soul'.

Picnic by Hanging Rock

Whitman:

I lassoo a sea-stack, corral illegal puffins' eggs and make a picnic. I feel the pull of box-beds, the tup-tup of mattock mattock, watch the tiny prick of lichen spore pit my carapace. In three millennia it will encrust me grey-greenly, blue-slately. Old Walt of Hoy, breaker of breakers! Lorca's still out there. He met me off the Brough of Birsay, turning the Earl's palace into a ruined leopard crouching in the sunlight, ready to pounce, to morsel me. Oh he's still out there, by the posse of little stacks, feeding the stone his sorrow, his hopeless loneliness. Only here five minutes and he's deserted me. Miserable boy! Moocher on machair! Just watch how I collapse his moulton-mini, origami it to lobster pot and pin him there. Or cramp him in creel cage, rope it with poney-blue rope and shush him through the fan-shaped netting of his mouth. He girns the slow Stromness girn of auburn hairweed streaming in the shallows of the apple-salmon sky. Or so *he* says, so *he* sings, mere boy of purple, yellow, cream coloured clover, the peace offerings he brings me in the night.

Whacky Races

In times of crisis, we must all decide again and again whom
we love
Frank O'Hara, 'To the Film Industry in Crisis'

Not you, Mel Gibson, with your sweet saltired face and mesomorphic buns, but you Stan and Ollie who tumble to a halt and land with a soft kerthump! on the grass of Rothiemurchus whose homophonous underlife suggests the tender mirth that lifted my mother for a second into adulthood the seconds after her first kiss. And there on the grass you spread the picnic cloth, take baby from the hamper while Ollie declares 'She says that I think more of you than I do of her!' and Stan: 'Well you do, don't you!' 'Well, we won't go into that' says Ollie and the 'Mmm! Mmm!' into his cress sandwich.

Not you Mel Gibson and the brusque inevitability of your courtships, but you Marlene Deitrich, golden Penelope Pitstop of all the lonely broughs and tidal causeways linking deserted Viking beaches of the Isles. You face square into the buffeting gale on Horgabost and breathe in the bachelor wind. You are a tiny spec of sand ghost shifting the sands of Selibost. You pedal on in your implausible Danish hoes sweeping the firths with the lugubrious vowels of your eyes.

Not you Mel Gibson with your slowmotionbagpipehorses but you, svelte and magnificent Peter Lorre whose internal whinnie blanches your face with that sweet-n'sour smile when you place your gloves on your top hat in such a particular way and suck on your stick of Edinburgh Rock as the attractive tourists admire your dual suspension Giant and we just know. We just know…

Not you Mel Gibson and your gratuitous splattering over the castle courtyard of an utterly dishy royal bumboy and paramour, thrown from the high windows of your prejudice, but you Cary Grant who have lept two feet from your saddle and quite unsettled Margaret Rutherford toppling beneath her basketful of Harris tweed with the news you've 'Just gone gay all of a sudden!'

Not you Mel Gibson but you openmouthed kissing, lustful embraces, sex perversion, seduction, nudity and even the occasional profanity. Not you Mel, but 'ain't this tasty shortbread! Wonder if ah could get the recipe. Sure would like to surprise ma maw when ah get back home' where 'Once I had a secret love / That lived within the heart of me' and he was 'the purtiest thing ah ever seen'. 'Say! That's a good looking gun you've got there. Can I see it? Maybe you'd like to see mine?'

But not the one used in all our murders, Mel, nor our suicides, our stabbings and chants of 'Kill her! Kill her! Kill her!' Or the trees that fall on you and the fire-

bombings and the burnings alive, the 'help!' that's screamed too late, the silent pity for the hanged one or the one we never see who everyone talks of and who dies like Frankenstein.

'Hey! I'm not a fag. I'm a werewolf!'

The Lochs of Scotland

Whitman:

Loveblows, Loch Vaich,
Loveblossoms, Loch Fleet
Loveclimbers Veyatie,
Loveverdure Maree,

Love Vines Fionn,
Lovebranches nan Uamh,
Loveroot Achonachie,
Climber-blossom Inch.

Verdure Morie,
Branch, fruit and vine.

Loveroot a' Chroisg,
Juice Climber Quoich,
Silk Crotch Lochy,
Crotch-bulb and vine.

Juicy Duich climbering mine.
Bulb, silk-thread-crotch
And Lochan Fada.

from *The Entomology of Scotland*

Family: Papilionidae – the Swallowtails and Apollos
Sub-Family: Despondentoso
Lorca apollo *(Linnaeus) Plate 32.11*
Status: Doubtfully Scottish
  Early 20th Century introduction, extinct resident or migrant
History: Only a single report of this butterfly in Scotland exists. This appears in the Entomologist's Weekly Intelligencer *(Vol. 12, no. 178, p.116, 1946):*

> Captured near Perth. – I take the liberty of sending you a list of my first month's recordable captures, in the Braes of Gowrie, near Kilspindie: Lorca apollo, fresh from ghost pupae, visiting marsh plants in a wood. *Edward Morgan, 28 June*

*Buchanan White was doubtful however (*Ent. Wkly. Intell. *Vol.13, no. 179, p.117, 1946):*

> The occurrence of Lorca apollo near Perth is problematical; from all that I can learn, I think some common Clouded Patersonian must have been mistaken for apollo. The captor was quite a novice, and as soon as he (as he thought) had ascertained the species, he flung the specimen away!

Habits: Despite its rather florid foreign-sounding name, Lorca is a timid creature with a weak flight. The larvae feed primarily on the Tuberous Pea (Lathyrus tuberosus). Those lucky enough to see it emerging from its chrysalis will hear its freshly beating wings make a sound similar to Spanish castanetes. It makes this sound twice only during its short life: once in the final stage of its metamorphosis and just prior to its extinction.

Form in Scotland: Unknown.

Fish Cakes and Bacon-Splendid

I, Walt, Prince of stone-skiffers,
Sit in Skarabrae portaloo,
Rocked by wind and more wind
And read the graffiti: 'HUNS ARE SHITE'.

I shite in Skarabrae portaloo
But am also buried under the stone dresser.
I sing from the abandoned limpet tank
And am the midden they built walls from,

Walt, the midden ancestor,
Passing the centuries through me,
Mulling over breakfast as I milled the sea
Through the harvesting spokes of my wheels.

I hail my breakfasting companion, Judge Steven Toomins,
Who sits in Steinigar Guest House with his lady wife
Chomping 'Fish cakes and bacon-splendid!'
Judge Toomins of the prison reform, Steven of the second buttery!

I salute you, expander of exiguity!
But ask you to accept the mitigating
Circumstance of Neolithic villagers,
Cell-penned by wind and sand.

I do not plead their case but ours:
Abrogate harsh prejudice in session
On this grassy verge a bench above
The excavated bedrooms of a stone-age house.

Look down upon us mercifully as we lie together,
Curled in the recessed box-beds, half-moons
Embracing sleep like the ancient dead of Maes Howe,
The grave treasure of our bicycles clicking over through the night.

Convoke the morning when our bones
And waking smiles make today's *Orcadian*.
How they marvel at our simple mysteries!
That we could be so like them yet so different,

So distant yet so present! O Toomins!
Do not exhibit or rebury us,
But leave us to cycle on our frail ash saddles
Over the stencilled shore.

Here are mock Skarabrae of local children
And a judgement written in sand:
'BANGLADESH I LOVE YOU'.

River Walt

Chasuble of water! Cope of bubbles, cope!
As River Walt bursts Tay banks and floods
Dunkeld's arbustes and grassy meads.
Walt waterfalls the spate, Leviathan surged
Up, shaking from shoulders
An atlas of Scottish burns and churches,
Douche of parchment, pearling
Abdomen and funny bones.

Inkdrop kings vault from his knees to
Blot a little beach, oakapple knights,
Inverted keeps earring the air and fall.
Firs bejewelled with names of places
He has been and is, speak, spoke and wheel
The ceaseless freshets of Cathedral lawns.
He moves and a Liliputian poet of the place,
Old Gavin Douglas, absails from his pockets

Down to bonkis, *a tiny, clanking, weeping*
Buke *clenched beneath his oxters;*
He turns, sprouts centuries from his stature
Then heaves Walt up behind him:
'My haund of bastyrd Latyn, beau schirr,
Or my haund of Scottis. Chuse.'
'O Scots Ulysses! Bishop of Translators!
I grasp a hand both changed and changing

Whose reticulated tracery flowers
In the bullseye fingernails of Scottish English.
For I am the ancestor and descendant
Of all afflatus and where I step the songlines
Of the places in which I do not have to ask
Make corroborees of land and water
Where men dreamtrack each other
Modulating shared melodies of difference.

Here is my friend, your kissing cousin,
The poet Lorca, who rides his Buster Keaton bike
Among the foreign cloisters of your charge.
Let his obscure, breezing wheels
Retain their Spanish accent and bless us,
Jumped-up fishes cycling to the ghost altar,
Altering the ache of spaces
In the uninhabited Scottish air.

We are the shimmering-slow progress forbears,
Protomartyrs of reid ryveris:
Our auncient vyces move this water,
Then still it in a nave of scalopped stone.
We arch before you, Gavin,
Our backs becoming candle-snuffer
Roofs, our skeletons dilating spokes
To form a window rose.

Behold our enlightened bones!
You hear us from your dreaming grave,
Ambulatory tyres in the crypt,
The buzz in the long-gone bee-boll,
The dip of ciborium bells.'

Spokes

Nervure or cantilever; striae or slick. Is that click-tick the sound of spokes, the graze of shin on chitinous pedals or freewheel forewings brushing the North Atlantic?

The Vallentino derailleur slips down a ring and the words fly out:

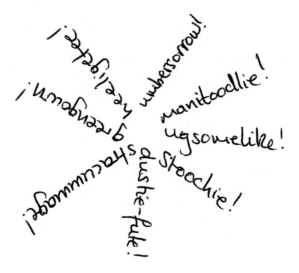

What do they translate? Sounds that help to root the songs of Yankee bike and Spanish butterfly? Fragments of the perfect imago *of Scotland that gaily jumps its chrysalis when they're neck and neck and fuse: Shimano Papilionidae.*

Rossignol

Whitman:

My Federico, my bird. Nightingale boy! There is a freeze of notes on every landing when I climb up to you. A struggling angel in each note. Filigree of curlicue warbling down its balustrade of tunes. Sound stencil of rapunzled hair. Grip! Check out that flash, that scoopy serpentine as you shimmy to your mirror fighting for the next phrase in your song! It's there! Already there! You're dancing moons off it in puddles on every European street. Each droplet of the Glasgow smir tiararing your bouffon hair is blessing, fierce smile of the angel as he reaches for your thigh. Listen! Deep in the goa trance of *Le Bar* my wings beat briefly about your strawberry beak. My lemon-blow mouth is on your neck, my rasping tongue finds ears wherever touch rests or taps. In the dull glow of leather I briefly abdicate, nibbling at feelings' edges and you ask again and again – destroyer, preserver – for a name, a number, the right to see my face again. Fairies de Norteamérica, Pajaros, La Habana, Rossignols de Paris and of Glasgow, it does not matter that I do not give it. It flutters in my eyes, in the throb of that small bird-bone in your thigh and when you wake, you wake up refreshed, the taste of silver-paper in your song, happy in unfamiliar cities or tender foreign plains.

Berriedale Wood

Whitman:

      To the tourist torched cinders of Berriedale Wood –
Ghost Aspen, Hazel, Rowan and Birch –
I bring gifts of American trees
Begin and end with leaves

Leaves alternate leaves simple leaves persistent
leaves linear, flattened, light green beneath

Lorca:

      At five in the afternoon
Berriedale Woodland fell
Ash of stipule
Velocities of fire

At five in the afternoon
I offer it plugs of dolerite
My arms of schistose rock.

Whitman:

      My lobes of leaves palmately lobed
Leaves stellate, pubescent,
Leaves orbicular to lanceolate
My knees of leaves and branchlets glabrous

Lorca:

      My albite-quartz veins
Alternating phyllites of Innellan
The North-West dip of Dunoon grits
Due to the inversion of my suicidal fire-escapes

Whitman:

      I am the White Pine and the Honey Locust,
The Screw Bean, The Kentucky Coffee-Tree.
Berriedale I lay my Horse Bean hands
On tortured roots, weep moist limestone soil
From the neighbourhood of Matagorda Bay.
I fertilise and stimulate and grow your most northerly woodland soil.

Lorca:

I am the Border Fault
Pebble of quartz and felspar
Little crystals of Colintraive
Hornblende of Glendaruel

Berriedale:

flowers of gneiss
fruit of long-winged samara and fruit a drupe, leaves aromatic when
bruised, leaves resinous-dotted, beard obtuse, eye-lash acute, leaves
more or less wedge-shaped at the base, cambrian crotch and sandstone
cedar, limestone juniper and hair, epidiorite pine, sill of black willow,
densely flowered staminate aments, villous freckles, freckled winter-buds
of mica

For willow oak of Cardross
I pay you rowan
For garnet acorn
Droppings of fossilized hazel

Web of footstep at five o'clock of the 20th of April lustrous of inland
Auchenhew of wing-margined above of hoary-tomentose of composite of
palm of hand of American and Spanish stone:

Rock-tree bodies that have walked in low wet woods on the borders of
streams and on dry hills in forests of Oak and Pine.

Tandem

Tandem of poets! Knights of the tandem!
As Walt and Federico birl away
What do you reply to the Lady of Surveys:
'How often do you cycle these paths?'
'Lady, O Lady! We *are* these paths!'
'And your income, beau schirrs, just point
To an appropriate band.' 'Our income,
Lady, is merl and mayvis and nychtyngale
With mery notis myrthfully furth brest
And our expenditure is goldspynk,
Lyntquhite, quytteris of skiffing wurds.'

FIFTH QUARTER

i.m. Derek Jarman

'If a garden isn't shaggy, forget it!' (DJ)

Invocation

Ariel, 'pearl of fire',
Clarified spirit –
(There is a mouseguard
On the beehive,
Safe: all
Golden things) –
Doodle, Ariel,
Inhumane, distracted,
Blood shingle by the shore
For water-courses
And shower us:
Derek in a wizard's hat
Spelling Dungeness sands

Super 8

In his childhood's manuscript,
Sparkles flowered: 'I remember
Daisies, words like *Zuassa*
And *Maggiore* that would not
Stiffen, even at the scent of lime.'

Like a crow you stole
All cinema's glistening
Detritus, hiding the tea-spoons,
The clothes-pegs,
The baking foil,
Pinning them to the santolina,
The helidrysum of the screen
Which chirrups at us
Like a silver jubilee.

Light banks
The cascades
Are quite worn through

Still

O bee-hat
Above a shepherd's crook
Herding pebbles
Into wiriness

to the solve of flood: a water hand, a sensitive hand churns in the waves. His palms kindle foam, an alchemy of bubbles, seeking soap stone, tearing with the roman vitriol of nails. Lightening palm, palm the colour of honey, white arsenic. Look! The serpent life-line, *originall of Nilus,* changes the sea into itself, its smoky blue, its seeded white, a finer bone, a fist of rivered veins. A man of vinegar is being born, of slow heat, quicklime, retort and potash. Saltpetre hand, hand of cinnebar and verdigris seeking the sun, here no there no it's water no air no light no flame no it's flower it's blue it's blue it's blue

From the sand
The gentle man
From the shell
The gentle boy
In cardigan
And Calvin Kleins
Breasting the surf
With down and tan
Beneath the sodden
Wool and cotton

His footprint warms
The winter beach
The grains beneath
The balls of feet
Swell slightly
To caress his
Firm instep

Ferdinand always
Ferdinand even
In the combat gear
Of shipwreck
Hair in place
Despite the Tempest
A strapping pet
Waterlogged but snoggable
Making for the dunes

Stills

Still speeding lens
Net against chest
Rope against
Chords of muscle

Windchimes

A verdigris trumpet

A dwarf pear

Er… A Tempest

'OK!ACTION! Right, whattawegot?' 'Shipwreck. Multiple facial abrasion, scalp lacerations, penetrating trauma to zone two of the neck. One… er… Caliban. No first name. BP's 98 over 60, pulse 92, reps 24. Moon calf floored by a thunder-stroke. No guarding or rebound tenderness, normal ball sounds. Log roll him. One, two, three! Admit axelary line.' 'Watayaseekid? Whatayasee? Pan in, pan in!' 'His arms betrims and thatch of meads, his stover sullied, liver trampled by live nibbling sheep, a gut of wheat, rye, barley, vetches, oats and pease but half-digested, traces of pyroxidine, carbamazepine, tracking though that watry arch now, formed by rib cage. Yes! A grass plot. There peacocks fly amain. I'm framing up his bosky acres and his uncrushed down. Amazing! What a montage! His spongy April is completely overgrown by broom-groves. This is one heck of a dismissèd bachelor! Focus on that waspish head embedded in his abdomen. Death was no honey-drop, soured refreshings. Scandalled company! poor guy. Have you ever seen such a blue bow, saffron wings, rich scarf, such a Caliban!'

Stills

Escaped periwinkle   Sulphudiazine   Laceflower

And Ariel of course
Is a little trowel
Who'll hatch
From the gentle
Bunch of Barry's
Forearm as he lifts
Fags from the corners
Of his mouth: for you
For me

Short

Dark slowly maps
The salt sea-marsh

Wave flows to wave;
Sunglut; a shell
Gloops and light
Is born through
A shinglequake

This is the fifth
Quarter of the globe
All outside is here
And he is at home

Glitters a dull pewter:
His hair

Prospect

nuff said

here: the reindeer moss

imagine   its dapples

...nuff heard

dodder or

muted rainbow

At every air
You are fenceless

och...nuff...

Rest-harrow
Beautiful and necessary
weed

Note: Derek Jarman, the British film director, died of AIDS in 1994. His films include *Jubilee, The Last of England, Caravaggio* and adaptations of Shakespeare's *The Tempest* and Marlowe's *Edward II*. During the final years of his life, he came to live in Prospect Cottage on the south coast of England near the Dungeness Power Station and created a remarkable garden out of this bleak, beautiful landscape. It is celebrated in his film *The Garden*.